B53 081 932 7

KT-144-770

PUZZLE HEROES

WILDLIFE WONDERS

ANNA NILSEN

ILLUSTRATED BY DAVE SMITH

This boo.

The loan n.
a further pe

www\

W
FRANKLIN WATTS
LONDON • SYDNEY

CONTENTS

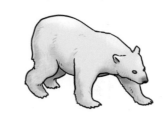

5 – 7 THE QUEST BEGINS

8 – 9 MADAGASCAR

10 – 11 UGANDA, AFRICA

12 – 13 THE GREAT BARRIER REEF, AUSTRALIA

14 – 15 THE AMAZON BASIN

16 – 17 THE ROCKY MOUNTAINS, NORTH AMERICA

18 – 19 THE ARCTIC

20 – 21 EUROPEAN WOODLAND

22 – 23 THE SAHARA DESERT

24 – 25 ENDANGERED CREATURES MAP

26 – 27 RANTHAMBORE, INDIA

28 – 31 ANSWERS

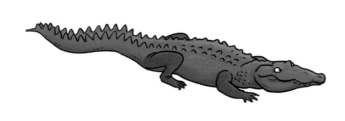

THE QUEST BEGINS

MEET THE CHARACTERS

 ZAK
 LEAH
 DAD
 MUM

Zak and Leah and their family are time – and space – travellers. Their mum is a wildlife photographer. She has been travelling around the world taking photos for a book on world wildlife.

I'll be your guide to the puzzles you have to solve.

MUM'S MAP

THE ARCTIC

EUROPE

RANTHAMBORE, INDIA

THE ROCKY MOUNTAINS

GREAT BARRIER REEF, AUSTRALIA

N
W   E
S

THE SAHARA DESERT

UGANDA, AFRICA

THE AMAZON BASIN

START HERE AT MADAGASCAR

MUM DISAPPEARS!

One day, Zak and Leah are at home with Dad when they receive a text message from Mum.

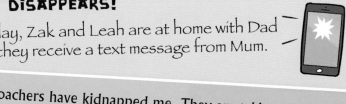

'Poachers have kidnapped me. They are taking me around the world so I can identify endangered animals for them. They are taking me to nine places but I don't know in what order yet. I've sent you a map with the places we are going to. I'm in Madagascar at the moment so I will leave you a trail of clues starting here. Each clue spells out the next place they are taking me to. Solve the anagram and go to the answer location next. Continue following the trail until you have been everywhere. I will leave you an object belonging to me at the end of trail so you will know where they have locked me up.'

ARE YOU A PUZZLE HERO?

The poachers sent Zak and Leah another message. It warned them that if they did not solve all the puzzles, they would not get Mum back. Can you help Zak, Leah and Dad solve all the puzzles and find Mum?

The parrot is your guide to the puzzles.

MUM'S PHOTOGRAPHY CHARTS

Mum should have recorded how many of each animal she photographed in each location. She's started it but has forgotten to finish it. Make a copy and complete the chart. Be sure you count the animals carefully.

Madagascar (pages 8–9)	Black lemur **1**	Brown lemur **4**	Madagascar flying fox **4**	Ring-tailed mongoose **2**	Ring-tailed lemur **10**	**21**
Uganda, Africa (pages 10–11)	Chimp	Jacana	Rhino	Kingfisher	Blue-headed tree agami	
Great Barrier Reef, Australia (pages 12–13)	Crown-of-thorns starfish	Crab	Giant clam	Clown trigger fish	Barramundi cod	
Amazon Basin (pages 14–15)	Capybara	Sloth	Potoo	Little woodstar hummingbird	Spider monkey	
Rocky Mountains, North America (pages 16–17)	Bison	Beaver	Bighorn sheep	Moose	Red squirrel	
Arctic (pages 18–19)	Arctic fox	Musk ox	Reindeer	Gyrfalcon	Harp seal	
European Woodland (pages 20–21)	European green lizard	Sand lizard	European green woodpecker	Roe deer	Wild cat	
Sahara Desert (pages 22-23)	Desert hare	Ostrich	Monitor lizard	Moula moula	Long-legged buzzard	
Ranthambore, India (pages 26–27)	White-throated kingfisher	Five-striped palm squirrel	Mongoose	Blue jay	Sloth bear	

PAN THE GOD OF NATURE AND ARTEMIS THE GODDESS OF WILD ANIMALS

Mum scattered charms of Pan, the Greek god of nature, and Artemis, the Greek goddess of wild animals, to leave a trail for Dad and the children to follow. To save Mum, you must check you have spotted them both in each place.

THE GREAT CHAMELEON HUNT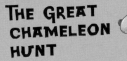

Zak and Leah brought their pet chameleon with them from an earlier adventure in Egypt. It has escaped again! Can you help Zak and Leah find it in each place (except in Madagascar)?

THE GREEN MAN

The Green Man motif is found in many cultures around the world. He is dressed to blend in with the natural world and is a symbol of the cycle of growth each spring. Can you find him in each place?

PUZZLE CLUES

DEADLY CREATURES

The poachers have left a trail of deadly creatures to try to stop Mum's rescue! There are several in each place. Can you spot them all before they kill Dad, Zak and Leah? Count them carefully to be sure you find them all.

MADAGASCAR
 Nile crocodile   Mosquito

AFRICA
 Hippo   Lion   Nile crocodile   Black mamba   Buffalo   Elephant   Mosquito

GREAT BARRIER REEF, AUSTRALIA
 Stone fish   Blue-ringed octopus   Box jellyfish

AMAZON BASIN
 Bullet ant   Mosquito   South American bushmaster   Brazilian wandering spider    Fer-de-lance

ROCKY MOUNTAINS
 Black widow spider

ARCTIC
 Polar bear

EUROPEAN FOREST
 Common European adder   Horn-nosed adder   Meadow viper   Brown bear   Asp viper

SAHARA DESERT
 Horned viper   Egyptian cobra    Death stalker scorpion

INDIA
 Tiger   Crocodile   Mosquito   King cobra

20-21 FOOD CHAINS PUZZLE

A food chain shows energy flow from one plant or animal to another. Plants are called primary producers because they make their own food from sunlight and are at the bottom of every food chain.

How many complete food chains can you find in the illustration on pages 20-21? Match each creature to one in the illustration. You can only use each creature or plant once although there may be extra creatures in the illustration that are not included in these food chains.

CHAIN 1	CHAIN 2	CHAIN 3	CHAIN 4	CHAIN 5	CHAIN 6
Soil	Plant	Plant	Grass	Dead vegetation	Blackberry
Worm	Rabbit	Centipede	Grasshopper	Woodlouse	Dormouse
Mole	Owl	Wild boar	Wolf spider	Woodlouse spider	Asp viper
Weasel	Wild cat	Wolf	Wasp	Shrew	Hawk
Fox	Weasel	Bear	Lizard	Owl	
Eagle	Hawk			Fox	

MORE TO FIND!

 Minibeasts – how many of each are there?

 Track puzzle – Help Zak or Leah follow the prints to find out who has made them.

MADAGASCAR

The island of Madagascar is off the east coast of Africa. Around 88 million years ago it broke off from the Indian continent. Its wildlife developed in isolation, with the result that over 80% of the species exist nowhere else on Earth.

COUNT AND SPOT CHAMELEONS
Chameleons are lizards that come in a range of colours.

Some chameleons can even change colour, for instance to give a signal of the mood they are in! The species also varies in size from 3 cm to 68 cm (the size of a cat). Nearly half of the 160 known chameleon species are found in Madagascar.

Can you find all the chameleons in the scene? Look carefully. You may spot the whole body or just a detail, like a curly tail or a swivelling eye.

SPIDER MAZE
Can you catch the huntsman spider in the web? Make your way from the Darwin's bark spider to the huntsman spider at the centre of the maze without jumping blocks or breaks in the web.

Darwin's bark spider

Huntsman spider

COUNT THE MINIBEASTS
How many of these minibeasts can you find?

Giant stick insect

Giraffe weevil

Comet moth

Malagasy green lynx spider

DEADLY CREATURES
How many of these deadly creatures can you spot?

Nile crocodile

Mosquito

Can you spot the Green Man?

WHOSE TRACKS ARE THESE?

Follow the tracks to find out who they lead to.

E

P

CAN YOU SPOT PAN AND ARTEMIS SOMEWHERE IN THIS PICTURE?

UGANDA, AFRICA

Uganda is a landlocked country in East Africa. It has ten national parks, over 300 different types of mammal and more than 1,000 species of bird. Uganda is also home to more than half of the world's mountain gorillas, which live high in the mountain forests.

 BODY PARTS
How many of these body parts can you spot in Uganda? Flip through the book to see where the other creatures live.

Beaks

Feet

Eyes

Tails

 GECKOES
How many chevron-throated dwarf geckoes can you find? Look carefully as they are well camouflaged.

 COUNT THE MINIBEASTS
How many of these minibeasts can you find?

Leaf bug   Flower beetle   Praying mantis

 **DEADLY CREATURES**
How many of these deadly creatures can you spot?

 Mosquito

   Buffalo

  Black mamba

Lion   Pygmy hippo

 Nile crocodile   Elephant

  Can you spot the Green Man?

 WHOSE TRACKS ARE THESE?
Follow the tracks to find out who they lead to.

THE GREAT BARRIER REEF, AUSTRALIA

The Great Barrier Reef is the world's largest coral reef system. It is in the Coral Sea, off the coast of Queensland, Australia. Corals are tiny sea animals. Most types of coral live in warm tropical oceans, where their skeletons form reefs.

There are many threats to the Great Barrier Reef including overfishing, global warming, tourism and pollution. According to new research, the reef has lost more than half its coral cover in the last 30 years.

 SPOT THE SHARKS AND TURTLES
Which of these sharks and turtles do not live on the Great Barrier Reef? (Search the picture to find out which of these are not there.)

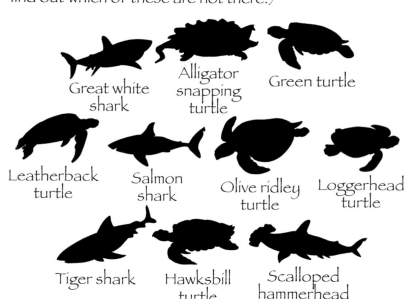

Great white shark

Alligator snapping turtle

Green turtle

Leatherback turtle

Salmon shark

Olive ridley turtle

Loggerhead turtle

Tiger shark

Hawksbill turtle

Scalloped hammerhead shark

 COUNT THE MINIBEASTS
How many of these minibeasts can you find?

Sea slugs

Sea cucumbers

Sea spiders

 DEADLY CREATURES
How many of these deadly creatures can you spot?

Stone fish

Blue-ringed octopus

Box jellyfish

 Can you spot the Green Man?

 **WHOSE TRACKS ARE THESE?**
Follow the tracks to find out who they lead to.

CAN YOU SPOT PAN AND ARTEMIS SOMEWHERE IN THESE PICTURES?

1. The Great Barrier Reef can be seen by astronauts from outer space and covers around 344,400 square kilometres.

4. Most fish have skeletons of bone but sharks are made of cartilage. Unlike fish, they have a backbone extending to the tip of the tail.

7. There are over 1,600 species of fish and 3,000 molluscs on the reef. Giant clams can grow to be more than one metre long and can be at least 70 years old.

2. It is made up of roughly 3,000 individual reefs and 600 islands. There are over 600 species of coral but many are threatened by coral disease and bleaching.

3. The crown-of-thorns starfish preys on coral. It releases the liquid from its stomach onto the coral. This liquid softens the coral and then the starfish eats it. One starfish can eat up to six square metres of living reef in a single year. The blue coral crab eats excess sediment from the coral and fends off the crown-of-thorns starfish.

6 The life span of the largest brain coral is 900 years. Colonies can grow as large as two metres around.

MiNi MAZE Conquer the brain maze to reach the red spot.

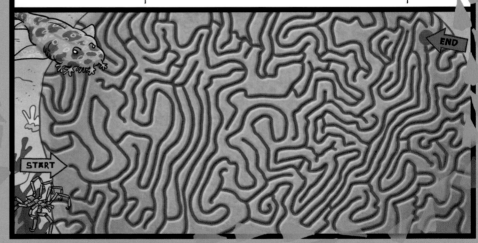

5. Sea snakes need to come up for air every 20 to 30 minutes. Their flattened tail acts as a paddle to make swimming easier.

8. The spiny seahorse changes colour to match its surroundings.

9. Fourteen species of sea snake live on the Great Barrier Reef. They have a poisonous bite to paralyse their prey. They feed on fish, eels and fish eggs. Some grow to over two metres in length.

CAN YOU SPOT PAN AND ARTEMIS SOMEWHERE IN THIS PICTURE?

THE AMAZON BASIN

The Amazon Basin is the part of South America that is drained by the River Amazon. Most of the area is covered by the world's largest rainforest, which covers around 5.5 million square kilometres. The basin extends across the countries of Bolivia, Brazil, Colombia, Ecuador, Guyana, Peru and Venezuela. More than 3,000 species of fish and over 1,300 species of bird live here.

I SPY FROGS AND TOADS

There are over 1,000 species of frog in the Amazon Basin. How many species of frog can you find?

THE OWL BUTTERFLY

There are over 1,000 species of butterfly. The owl butterfly has large 'eyes' just like an owl. The pupa looks like a dried leaf hanging on a branch. How many pupae and owl butterflies can you spot?

Pupa of owl butterfly

COUNT THE MINIBEASTS
How many of each of these minibeasts can you count?

Giant Amazonian carrion scarab beetle

Jumping spider

Leaf-cutter ant

Goliath bird-eating tarantula

DEADLY CREATURES
How many of each of these can you spot?

Bullet ant

Mosquito

The Brazilian wandering spider

Fer-de-lance

South American bushmaster

Can you spot the Green Man?

WHOSE TRACKS ARE THESE?
Follow the footprints to discover which creature made them.

THE ROCKY MOUNTAINS, NORTH AMERICA

The Rocky Mountains stretch from British Columbia, in western Canada, down to New Mexico, in the USA. They are more than 4,800 kilometres long. The Rockies are home to a great deal of wildlife, such as elk, moose, white-tailed deer, pronghorns, mountain goats, bighorn sheep, black bears, grizzly bears, coyotes, lynxes and wolverines.

LOST MIGRATION PUZZLE
Animals who migrate move from one place to another as the seasons change. Who got lost on their migration and ended up in the Rocky Mountains by mistake? Who got lost migrating from the Rocky Mountains and where did they end up by mistake? Compare this scene with the other eight scenes in the book (leaving out the map on pages 24-25) to spot the matching animals. There are ten animals in all to find.

PUZZLING PIECES
How many of these jigsaw pieces come from the Rocky Mountains? Where do the others come from?

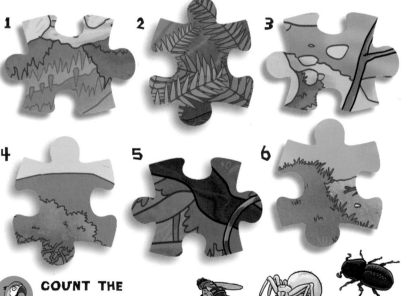

1
2
3
4
5
6

COUNT THE MINIBEASTS
How many of these minibeasts can you find?

Drone fly

Yellow spider

Mountain pine beetle

DEADLY CREATURES
How many of these deadly black widow spiders can you find?

Can you spot the Green Man?

WHOSE TRACKS ARE THESE?

Follow the tracks to find out who they lead to.

CAN YOU SPOT PAN AND ARTEMIS SOMEWHERE IN THIS PICTURE?

A

N

THE ARCTIC

The Arctic is in the northern most part of the Earth. The Arctic region consists of a vast, ice-covered ocean, surrounded by treeless land which is below freezing point. Many cold-blooded creatures have a natural anti-freeze in their blood to protect them from the damage that the cold temperatures would cause.

THE LONGEST SLEIGH RACE

Find out which sleigh went the furthest by using a piece of string to measure each sleigh's distance. Lay the string along the tracks of each sleigh and make a knot for each one. Which colour won?

FLYING BIRDS

How many of each of these birds can you spot in the sky? (Some aren't in the sky at all!)

Long-tailed duck

Snow goose

American kestrel

Arctic tern

Horned puffin

Tundra swan

Bald eagle

Snowy owl

CAN YOU SPOT PAN AND ARTEMIS SOMEWHERF IN THIS PICTURE?

 COUNT THE MINIBEASTS
How many of each of these minibeasts can you find?

 Arctic beetle

Arctic sea spider

Arctic wolf spider

 DEADLY CREATURES
How many of these deadly creatures can you spot?

 Polar bear

Polar bear cubs

 SNOW SCULPTURES
How many snow animals has Dad made in the snow for Zak and Leah?

 Can you spot the frozen Green Man?

 WHOSE TRACKS ARE THESE?
Follow the tracks to find out who they lead to.

EUROPEAN WOODLAND

Wildwoods used to cover most of Europe. Although most of them have been cleared for farming, housing or businesses, about 25% of the land is still covered by woodland or forest. Woodlands provide many different habitats for wildlife.

BURROWING MAZE

You are a worm trying to reach the surface and avoid being eaten by badgers. Can you find your way through the maze of tunnels and escape to the surface?

START

END

FOOD CHAINS

Every living thing needs energy to live. The sun gives energy to plants so they can grow. Some insects, birds and animals eat plants and some eat other animals. Use the chart on page 7 to find five complete food chains in the picture. Which one is incomplete?

COUNT THE MINIBEASTS

How many of each of these minibeasts can you find?

 Speckled wood

Centipede

 Hummingbird hawk-moth

Stag beetle

DEADLY CREATURES

How many of each of these deadly creatures can you spot?

 Asp viper

Brown bear

 Meadow viper

 Nose-horned viper

 Common European adder

Can you spot the Green Man?

WHOSE TRACKS ARE THESE?

Follow the tracks to find out who they lead to.

THE SAHARA DESERT

The Sahara is one of the hottest places on Earth and is the third largest desert in the world. It stretches over most of North Africa. It consists of large areas of barren rock, sand dunes and sand seas. The sand dunes can reach heights of 180 metres.

SPOT THE DIFFERENCE: NOCTURNAL ANIMALS

Nocturnal animals are only active at night. They are still out as dawn breaks (on page 22) but have disappeared to sleep on page 23, as the hot sun comes up. Compare the pictures to work out how many nocturnal animals are shown on page 22.

OSTRICH EGG PUZZLE

Examine the pieces of ostrich egg on page 22. How many complete eggs can you find with no missing pieces? If you're stuck, trace the pieces, cut them out and put them back together like a jigsaw puzzle. The first one on the right has been done for you!

SAND SCULPTURES
Dad has been sculpting again! How many sand sculptures can you spot on page 23? Look carefully as they are well camouflaged against the sand dunes.

COUNT THE MINIBEASTS
How many of each of these minibeasts can you find?

Dung beetle

Desert ant

Locust

DEADLY CREATURES
How many of each of these deadly creatures can you spot?

Egyptian cobra

Death stalker scorpion

Horned viper

  Can you spot the Green Man?

WHOSE TRACKS ARE THESE?
Follow the tracks to find out who they lead to.

23

Speech bubble: CAN YOU SPOT PAN AND ARTEMIS SOMEWHERE IN THIS PICTURE?

ENDANGERED CREATURES MAP

Zak and Leah must be on the right path... they've found Mum's map of the world's endangered creatures. Endangered creatures are those whose numbers are so small that they are at risk of extinction. Factors that threaten endangered creatures include loss of habitat, water scarcity, erosion, pollution, climate change, overfishing, oil and gas development and the illegal wildlife trade.

Endangered animals are marked on Mum's map - 19 of the animals on the map appear elsewhere in the book. Can you find them?

EXTINCT BIRDS

An extinct creature is one that no longer exists. You may be able to see them in museums as stuffed animals. Search the map of endangered creatures to see which of these birds is now extinct (they don't appear on the map).

Californian condor

Great auk

Hawaiian duck

Egyptian vulture

Dodo

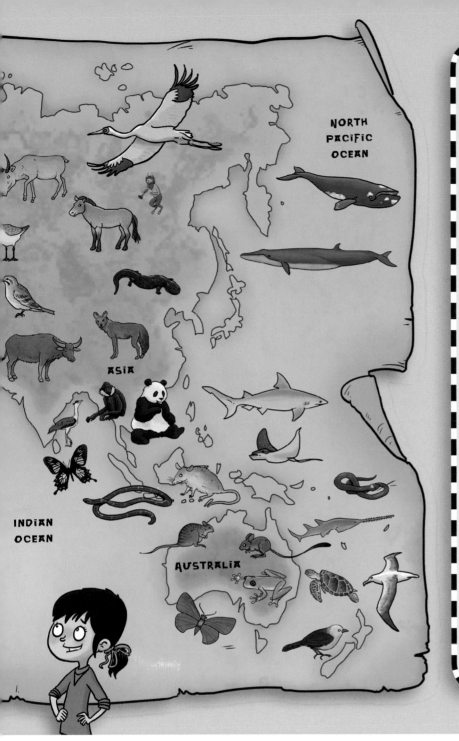

NORTH PACIFIC OCEAN

ASIA

INDIAN OCEAN

AUSTRALIA

WHERE IN THE WORLD?

Look back through the book and see if you can spot these creatures to discover where they live.

 Humphead wrasse

 Whooping crane

 Blue whale

 Slender-horned gazelle

 Silky sifaka

 Gorilla

 White-bellied heron

 Yellow-head parrot

SPOT THE MINIBEASTS

Three of these butterflies are endangered. Which ones?

 Queen Alexandra's birdwing

 Gaudy commodore

 Illidge's ant-blue

 Blue clipper

 Monarch

 Sri Lankan swallowtail

DEADLY CREATURES

Search the map to work out which of these deadly creatures is endangered.

 Polar bear

 Fire ant

 Golden poison frog

 Fiji snake

 Scalloped hammerhead shark

 Can you spot the Green Man?

25

RANTHAMBORE, INDIA

Ranthambore National Park is one of the biggest national parks in Northern India. It used to be a favourite hunting ground for the Maharajas (ruling princes) of Jaipur. It is now famous for its commitment to care for around 40 tigers who stroll around the protected site.

TIGERS AND DEER

How many tigers and deer can you spot? If each tiger catches one deer for supper, how many tigers will go without food?

SILHOUETTES

How many of each silhouetted creature can you spot?

Indian porcupine

Grey langur

Indian flying fox

Leopard

Jackal

COUNT THE MINIBEASTS

How many of each of these minibeasts can you find?

Indian leaf butterfly

Click beetle

Brahmeid moth

Camel spider

DEADLY CREATURES

How many of each of these deadly creatures can you spot?

Indian king cobra

Crocodile

Mosquito

 Can you spot the Green Man?

WHOSE TRACKS ARE THESE?

Follow the tracks to find out who they lead to.

26

27

ANSWERS

The pictures show you the best routes for the mazes. If you can't find Pan and Artemis or all the minibeasts and deadly creatures, and the chameleon, have another go!

8 – 9 MADAGASCAR

CHAMELEONS
There are 12 to find.

MINIBEASTS
Giant stick insect: 1
Giraffe weevil: 3
Comet moth: 2
Malagasy green lynx spider: 4

DEADLY CREATURES
Nile crocodile: 2
Mosquito: 4

SPOT THE GREEN MAN

WHOSE TRACKS ARE THESE?
Eastern lesser bamboo lemur

HOW MANY SNAKES ARE THERE?
(PAGE 27 PUZZLE):
4

10 – 11 UGANDA, AFRICA

The ones with ticks appear in Uganda.

Beaks

Shoebill stork

Toucan (Amazon Basin)   Eagle (The Rocky Mountains)   Saddlebill stork

Feet

Grey crowned crane   Clawed frog

Eyes

Greater Madagascar green tree frog (Madagascar)   Secretary bird

Tails

Five-lined skink (Rocky Mountains)   Giant pangolin   Giraffe

MUM'S PHOTOGRAPHY CHART
Chimp: 1; Jacana: 4; Rhino: 5;
Kingfisher: 3; Blue-headed tree agami: 1

TOTAL: 14

GECKOES
There are 3 to find.

MINIBEASTS
Leaf bug: 1
Flower beetle: 5
Praying mantis: 2.

DEADLY CREATURES
Lion: 2
Black mamba: 5
Nile crocodile: 5
Pygmy hippo: 9
Buffalo: 4
Mosquito: 7
Elephant: 1

SPOT THE GREEN MAN

WHOSE TRACKS ARE THESE?
Elephant

HOW MANY SNAKES ARE THERE?
(PAGE 27 PUZZLE):
13

12 – 13 THE GREAT BARRIER REEF, AUSTRALIA

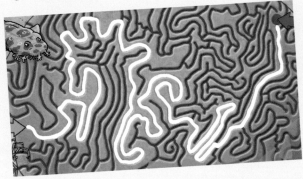

SPOT THE SHARKS AND TURTLES
The salmon shark and the alligator snapping turtle do not live on the Great Barrier Reef.

MINIBEASTS
Sea slug: 3
Sea cucumber: 5
Sea spider: 3

DEADLY CREATURES
Stone fish: 3
Blue-ringed octopus: 1
Box jellyfish: 2

SPOT THE GREEN MAN

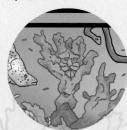

WHOSE TRACKS ARE THESE?
Human diver

HOW MANY SNAKES ARE THERE?
(PAGE 27 PUZZLE):
10

MUM'S PHOTOGRAPHY CHART
Crown-of-thorns Starfish : 3; Crab: 1;
Giant clam: 1; Clown trigger fish: 1
Barramundi cod: 4

TOTAL: 10

14 — 15 THE AMAZON BASIN

I SPY FROGS AND TOADS
There are 10 different frogs to find.

THE OWL BUTTERFLY
Pupa: 3; The owl butterfly: 4.

MINIBEASTS
Giant Amazonian carrion scarab beetle: 2; Jumping spider: 3
Leaf-cutter ant: 10
Goliath bird-eating tarantula: 1.

DEADLY CREATURES
Bullet ant: 10;
The Brazilian wandering spider: 1
Mosquito: 7; Fer-de-lance: 3
South American bushmaster: 2

SPOT THE GREEN MAN

WHOSE TRACKS ARE THESE?
Jaguar

HOW MANY SNAKES ARE THERE?
(PAGE 27 PUZZLE):
10

MUM'S PHOTOGRAPHY CHART
Capybara: 2; Sloth: 1; Potoo: 3
Little woodstar hummingbird: 4
Spider monkey: 2

TOTAL: 12

16 — 17 THE ROCKY MOUNTAINS, NORTH AMERICA

LOST MIGRATION PUZZLE
Who got lost migrating and ended up in Canada by mistake?

- Nightingale from Europe
- Wildebeest from Africa
- Zebra from Africa
- Aardvark from Africa
- Whale from Australia

Who got lost migrating from Canada?

- Canada Goose lost in Amazon
- Snow Goose lost in Madagascar
- Rufous hummingbird lost in Europe
- American Buffalo lost in India
- Caribou lost in the Sahara desert

PUZZLING PIECES
- Rocky Mountains pieces: 1, 3 and 6.
- Piece 2 from Europe, page 21;
- Piece 4 from India, page 27;
- Piece 5 the Amazon Basin, page 15.

MINIBEASTS
Yellow spider: 5
Drone fly: 2
Mountain pine beetle: 4

DEADLY CREATURES
Black widow spider: 5

SPOT THE GREEN MAN

WHOSE TRACKS ARE THESE?
North American porcupine

HOW MANY SNAKES ARE THERE?
(PAGE 27 PUZZLE):
6

MUM'S PHOTOGRAPHY CHART
Bison: 1; Beaver: 3; Bighorn sheep: 2
Moose: 1; Red squirrel: 2

TOTAL: 9

18 — 19 THE ARCTIC

THE LONGEST SLEIGH RACE
1st Red; 2nd Blue; 3rd Green; 4th Yellow

SNOW SCULPTURES
There are 5 snow sculptures.

MINIBEASTS
Arctic beetle: 4
Arctic sea spider: 3
Arctic wolf spider: 2

DEADLY CREATURES
Polar bears: 6
Polar bear cubs: 3

SPOT THE GREEN MAN

WHOSE TRACKS ? ARE THESE?
Arctic hare

HOW MANY SNAKES ARE THERE?
(PAGE 27 PUZZLE):
0

FLYING BIRDS
Long-tailed duck: 0; Snow goose: 3; American kestrel: 0;
Arctic tern: 5; Horned puffin: 0; Tundra swan: 4
Bald eagle: 0; Snowy owl: 2.

MUM'S PHOTOGRAPHY CHART
Arctic fox: 4; Musk ox: 3; Reindeer: 5;
Gyrfalcon: 2; Harp seal: 6

TOTAL: 20

20 — 21 EUROPEAN WOODLAND

BURROWING MAZE

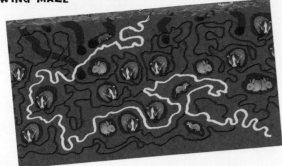

FOOD CHAINS
Number 4 is incomplete. The grasshopper is missing.

MINIBEASTS
Speckled wood: 2
Centipede: 1
Hummingbird hawk-moth: 1
Stag beetle: 2

DEADLY CREATURES
Common European adder: 2
Nose-horned viper: 1
Meadow viper: 2
Asp viper: 1
Brown bear: 2

SPOT THE GREEN MAN

WHOSE TRACKS ARE THESE?
Dormouse

HOW MANY SNAKES ARE THERE? (PAGE 27 PUZZLE):
12

MUM'S PHOTOGRAPHY CHART
European green lizard: 3; Sand lizard: 4;
European green woodpecker: 2; Roe deer: 1; Wild cat: 3
TOTAL: 13

---

22 — 23 THE SAHARA DESERT

SPOT THE DIFFERENCE: NOCTURNAL ANIMALS
There are 10 nocturnal animals:

Fennec fox | Death stalker scorpion | The pale fox | Egyptian cobra | Jerboa

Desert hedgehog | Spotted hyena | Saharan cheetah | Sand viper | Rüppels fox

OSTRICH EGG PUZZLE

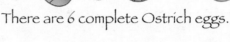

There are 6 complete Ostrich eggs.

SAND SCULPTURES
There are 4 sand sculptures on page 23.

SPOT THE GREEN MAN

WHOSE TRACKS ARE THESE?
Jerboa

MINIBEASTS
Dung beetle: 10
Desert ant: 23
Locust: 12

DEADLY CREATURES
Egyptian cobra: 2
Death stalker scorpion: 5
Horned viper: 3

HOW MANY SNAKES ARE THERE? (PAGE 27 PUZZLE):
7

MUM'S PHOTOGRAPHY CHART
Desert hare: 4; Ostrich: 5
Monitor lizard: 4; Moula moula: 3
Long legged buzzard: 4
TOTAL: 20

---

24 — 25 ENDANGERED CREATURES MAP

SPOT THE ENDANGERED CREATURES IN THE BOOK

MADAGASCAR (PAGES 8-9)

Indri

UGANDA (PAGES 10-11)

Grevy's zebra | African wild dog | Chimpanzee

AUSTRALIA (PAGES 12-13)

Longheaded eagle ray | Green turtle | Green sawfish

AMAZON BASIN (PAGES 14-15)

Golden-headed lion tamarin | The hoary-throated spinetail | Hyacinth macaw

ROCKY MOUNTAINS (PAGES 16-17)

Black footed ferret | Golden-cheeked warbler

ARCTIC (PAGES 18-19)

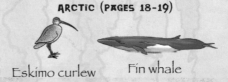

Eskimo curlew | Fin whale

EUROPEAN WOODLAND (PAGES 20-21)

European mink

SAHARA (PAGES 22-23)

Addax | Dama gazelle

RANTHAMBORE INDIA (PAGES 26-27)

Indian water buffalo | Great Indian bustard